Cursive Handwriting Practice

WORKBOOK *for* ADULTS

JULIE HARPER

Cursive Handwriting Practice Workbook for Adults

Education & Reference > Language Arts

ISBN 10: 1981274782

EAN 13: 978-1981274789

Table of Contents

Relaxation

Introduction

This cursive handwriting practice workbook is designed for adults (or teens).
- ✓ It uses a smaller font size than standard children's writing books.
- ✓ The blank lines are narrower than standard children's writing books.
- ✓ This book has a relaxing theme which may appeal more to adults.
- ✓ There is just a quick refresher of basic letter and word practice.
- ✓ Most pages aren't designed to be traced prior to copying.
- ✓ One chapter challenges you to rewrite printed sentences in cursive.
- ✓ The last chapter includes creative writing prompts.

The goal of this workbook is to provide adults an opportunity to learn or review cursive handwriting skills with an age-appropriate workbook. The first chapter provides a quick review of how to write each letter and offers a little practice writing individual letters. If you need more practice writing individual letters or single words, you may benefit from using this workbook in combination with a basic cursive writing workbook which focuses on more basic techniques.

May you improve your handwriting skills and enjoy reading and writing these relaxation-themed sentences.

Uppercase Cursive Alphabet

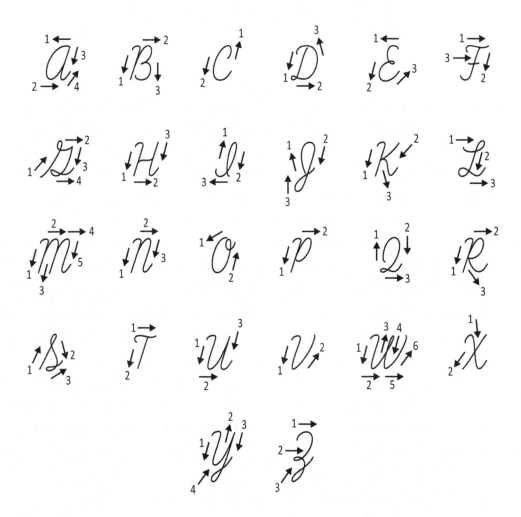

The arrows are included as a recommendation for how to write the cursive letters.

Lowercase Cursive Alphabet

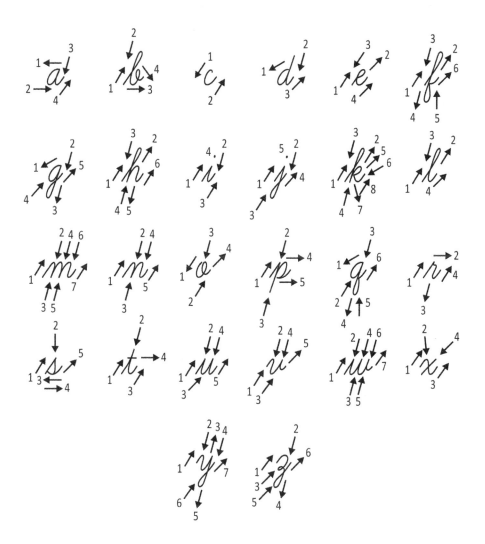

The arrows are included as a recommendation for how to write the cursive letters.

 Peace and Quiet

1

Quick Letter Review

Instructions: Trace each dotted letter and copy it onto the blank line below.

A A B B C C D D E E F F

a a b b c c d d e e f f

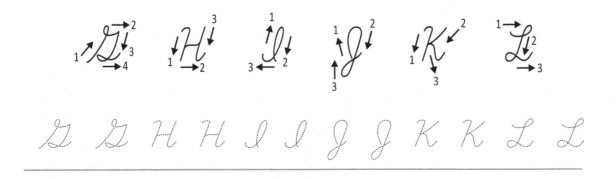

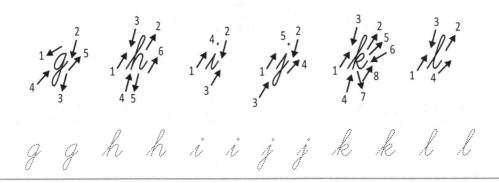

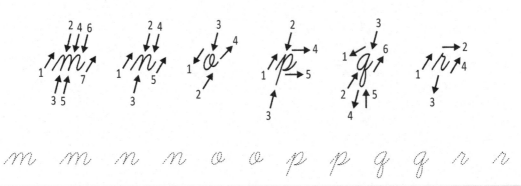

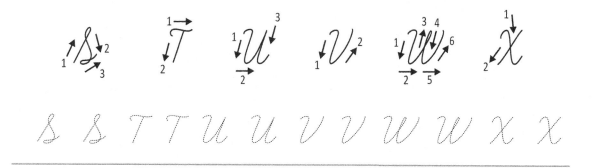

S S T T U U V V W W X X

s s t t u u v v w w x x

y y z z

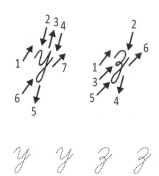

y y z z

Aa Bb Cc Dd Ee Ff Gg

Hh Ii Jj Kk Ll Mm Nn

Oo Pp Qq Rr Ss Tt Uu Vv

Ww Xx Yy Zz Aa Bb Cc Dd

Ee Ff Gg Hh Ii Jj Kk Ll

Mm Nn Oo Pp Qq Rr Ss

Tt Uu Vv Ww Xx Yy Zz

Aa Bb Cc Dd Ee Ff Gg

Hh Ii Jj Kk Ll Mm Nn

Oo Pp Qq Rr Ss Tt Uu Vv

Ww Xx Yy Zz Aa Bb Cc Dd

Ee Ff Gg Hh Ii Jj Kk Ll

Mm Nn Oo Pp Qq Rr Ss

Tt Uu Vv Ww Xx Yy Zz

A a B b C c D d E e F f G g

H h I i J j K k L l M m N n

O o P p Q q R r S s T t U u V v

W w X x Y y Z z A a B b C c D d

E e F f G g H h I i J j K k L l

M m N n O o P p Q q R r S s

T t U u V v W w X x Y y Z z

A a B b C c D d E e F f G g

H h I i J j K k L l M m N n

O o P p Q q R r S s T t U u V v

W w X x Y y Z z A a B b C c D d

E e F f G g H h I i J j K k L l

M m N n O o P p Q q R r S s

T t U u V v W w X x Y y Z z

 Ocean Breeze

2

Letter Blends

Cursive handwriting "blends" letters together. This allows you to write an entire word quickly without lifting your pencil from the page.

The following lowercase letters gain a little connector when they follow another letter.

a c d g o q

For example, compare the letter "o" in the two words below.

ocean o / moon o

The following uppercase letters don't connect with a lowercase letter that comes after it.

B D F O P T V W

For example, examine the first two letters in each of the words below.

Wisdom / Experience

Instructions: Trace each letter or word and copy it onto the blank line below.

Ac ac ac Ac ac ac Ac ac ac Ac ac ac

Achieve accomplish Actual account

Ap ap ap Ap ap ap Ap ap ap Ap ap ap

Appreciate apart Appropriate appointment

Be be be Be be be Be be be Be be be

Belief benefit Beauty best Being beam

Br br br Br br br Br br br Br br br

Breathe bright Bring brain Break brand

Ch ch ch Ch ch ch Ch ch ch Ch ch ch

Challenge champion Chocolate cheerful

Co co co Co co co Co co co Co co co

Courage confirm Compromise compete

Dr dr dr Dr dr dr Dr dr dr Dr dr dr

Dream dry Draw drift Drip drag

Ex ex ex Ex ex ex Ex ex ex Ex ex ex

Exist extraordinary Exhilarating excuse

Fa fa fa Fa fa fa Fa fa fa Fa fa fa

Fascinating fancy Fantastic fabulous

Gl gl gl Gl gl gl Gl gl gl Gl gl gl

Glad glance Glee glory Glide glue

Hu hu hu Hu hu hu Hu hu hu

Human hunt Humorous humble

Is is is Is is is Is is is Is is is

Island isolated Issues isthmus

Je je je Je je je Je je je Je je je

Jewel jelly Jest jeep Jet jeans Jealousy

Ki ki ki Ki ki ki Ki ki ki Ki ki ki

Kindness kiss Kingdom kidding

Lo lo lo Lo lo lo Lo lo lo Lo lo lo

Loveable longing Lookout lounge

Ma ma ma Ma ma ma Ma ma ma

Magnificent majestic Mature many

Ne ne ne Ne ne ne Ne ne ne Ne ne ne

Necessary needful Negotiate near

Oc oc oc Oc oc oc Oc oc oc Oc oc oc

Ocean occurrence Occasional occupied

Pr pr pr Pr pr pr Pr pr pr Pr pr pr

Promising professional Praise privilege

Qu qu qu Qu qu qu Qu qu qu Qu qu qu

Qualified quality Quiet questionable

Re re re Re re re Re re re Re re re

Relaxation rest Realistic refreshing

Sp sp sp Sp sp sp Sp sp sp Sp sp sp

Special space Springtime spiritually

St st st St st st St st st St st st

Steady straight Strong stupendous

Th th th Th th th Th th th Th th th

Thanks think Thoughtful through

Un un un Un un un Un un un

Unique understand Unusual unanimous

Va va va Va va va Va va va Va va va

Vacation values Valid Valuable

Wo wo wo Wo wo wo Wo wo wo

Wonderful world Woman worthy

Xy ax Ye ye Za za Xy ex Ye ye Ze ze

Xylophone axe Yes year Zest zeal

 Island Breeze

3

Words and Sentences

Instructions: Copy the words onto the blank line below.

(This section is not designed for tracing.)

Arts and artistic ability, aromatherapy, active

Beautiful bright butterflies, buzzing bumble bees

Composed, confident, cool, calm, and collected

Dazzling doodle designs, delightful drawings

Excellent, engaging, exquisite, effortless, encouraging

Fabulous, fine, fun, flourishing, family, friends

Generous, great, genuine, grinning, giving, giggling

Happy heart, helping hand, heavenly, harmonious

Idyllic, imagination, innovative, inspiring, ideal

Jazzy, jovial, joyous, jolly, jubilant, just, jointly

Kindheartedness, kindly, knowing, keen, kiss

Lackadaisical, lighthearted, loving, loyal

Majestic, merit, marvelous, meaningful, motivate

Needed, nice, nestled, nurturing, natural, now, new

Outback, outdoors, open, open-minded, optimistic

Paradise, poetry, peppy, pleasant, productive, proud

Quality, quiet, quantify, quest, qualified, quaint

Read, relax, rest, radiant, receptive, respectful

Singing songs, sunny, super special, splendorous

Thankful, touching, thoughtful, teamwork, tranquil

Useful, unity, upbeat, understanding, ultra, useful

Valued, visualized, vibrant, valuable, victory, vivid

Warmhearted, wonderland, whistle, wisdom, wow

X-tra, exquisite, excellent, excel, relax, flexible

Yoga, young-at-heart, yes, yummy, yeah, yahoo

Zany, zesty, zippy, zeal, zestful, zealous, zest, zip

Aromatherapy essential oils are used for relaxation.

Breathe easy for relaxation and calm feelings.

Creative arts help to encourage self-expression.

Dance to refresh yourself and feel energized.

Exercising to relax and improve our overall mood.

Find time to spend with family.

Gardening produces beauty while releasing stress.

Hug a friend to reduce stress levels.

Inspirational images help to relax the mind.

Jolly, jovial and just for fun.

Knitting something beautiful is always appreciated.

Laughing and giggling out loud is contagious.

Meditate with music to help relax after a busy day.

Need a break? Take time for yourself!

Out in the open country enjoying the fresh air.

Peace and quiet time to slow down and feel refreshed.

Quality time with family and friends is rewarding.

Reflexology massage may decrease stress.

Stop to smell the flowers and enjoy life.

Take it easy, resting and relaxing.

Unwind, relax, enjoy life!

Volunteer your time, skill, expertise or talent.

Write down the things you are thankful for.

"Xtra" relaxing lazy day today.

Young at heart? You bet!

Zesty and zippy.

Enjoy the great outdoors. Sit back and relax.

Listen to the sounds of nature. Hear the birds sing.

Hear the laughter of children having fun playing.

Enjoy the different outdoor aromas.

Smell the roses, pine trees, and fragrant flowers.

Step outside at night and go star gazing.

Enjoy the wonders of nature.

Find time to sit quietly and unwind.

Enjoy a breath of fresh air.

Allow yourself to relax and be calm.

Light a candle. Sip a cup of herbal green tea.

Clear your mind of all negative thoughts.

Yoga poses can help to relieve stress.

Breathe gently and relax.

Imagine lying in a hammock.

Hear ocean waves splash against the shore.

Feel a cool breeze blowing gently.

Enjoy the colorful display of a glorious sunset.

Immerse yourself in an amazing story.

Savor each bite of a delicious meal.

Unwind while taking a long bubble bath.

 Refreshments

4

Write Paragraphs

Instructions: Copy each paragraph onto the blank lines below.

The layout is designed so that you may write on every other line.

See the example below.

Helping others can be rewarding. You can be somebody's ray of sunshine.

Helping others can be rewarding. You can be somebody's ray of sunshine.

Dancing provides a good cardio workout. Like any exercise, dancing helps to reduce stress. If you enjoy the dance, it will feel like fun (not work). You can choose to dance in the privacy of your own home. Find a dance style that suits you well.

Listening to music can be a relaxing experience. An alternative to listening to music is to listen to sounds made by nature. A variety of water sounds – such as raindrops, waterfalls, or the splash of ocean waves – have a calming effect on some people.

When spring arrives, birds fill the air with happy songs. Tulips, daffodils, crocuses, and other bulbs begin to flower. Trees sprout new leaves. The days start to get longer, allowing us to spend more time outdoors enjoying the many wonders of nature.

Summertime lets you replace your boots with flip flops, and put the jackets and sweaters in storage. It's a chance to open windows and let fresh air in. Smell the sweet aroma of the blooming lilacs and other flowers. Watermelon makes a great summer snack.

Enjoy the cool crisp air when fall arrives. Chrysanthemums are blooming. Watch the leaves change to yellow, orange, and red colors. Soon the leaves will fall and the trees will be bare. Freshly baked pies fill the kitchen with warmth and pleasant aromas.

Winter is the coldest season, but the family can still enjoy outdoor activities such as sledding, skiing, or ice skating. If it snows, watch children make snowmen or throw snowballs. Get cozy and snuggle up next to a fireplace to keep warm.

Coloring is not just for kids. It is also a
fun way to help adults relieve stress.
There are hundreds of coloring books
specifically designed for adults. Have a
coloring party where everyone is a
winner. It can be fun, relaxing, and
an enjoyable way to socialize.

Choose a coloring book that allows you to color pictures of things that interest you, such as flowers, butterflies, or mandalas. Use colored pencils, gel pens, colored markers, or crayons to complete your picture. Your mind and body may appreciate the calming benefits.

Exercising with a friend can be fun. You can offer each other inspiration and motivation. Bringing a friend can help you try something that you would feel uncomfortable doing alone. Challenge each other to see how quickly you can meet your goals.

Relax your muscles in a hot tub, sauna, or jacuzzi. Enjoy the therapeutic benefits of a hot tub bath. Let the spa relax your tired muscles. Revitalize your mind and body in a natural hot spring. Ancient cultures used spas and springs for relaxation and therapy.

Remember what it was like to be a child. Rediscover your sense of wonder. Try to see things as if you're seeing them for the first time. Enjoy little things that we often take for granted. Put your worries aside for a while and have a little carefree fun.

Do any fond memories come to mind?
Can you remember good childhood
moments? What fun things have you
done with your friends? Have you ever
won any type of contest? Did you ever
visit a special place? Which memories
make you smile?

According to research, reading is one of the best and fastest ways to relax your mind. A few minutes of reading can lower your stress level. This is one more reason to curl up and read a good book. Let your mind escape to where the book takes you.

Nature offers a wide variety of textures, sights, sounds, and aromas. Have you ever rubbed your fingers against moss or the bark on a tree? Imagine the sound of a waterfall. Remember smells from a garden. Enjoy the colorful display of a sunset or rainbow.

There are many ways to pay it forward. It could be a little thing like holding the door open for a stranger. You could donate clothing you no longer wear. Give something you don't need to someone who may appreciate it. Small acts of kindness often bring smiles.

Volunteering and giving back to others benefits both mental and physical health. It can provide one with a sense of purpose, and is a good way to be more socially connected. If you help to clean up a local park, your body will benefit from the exercise.

Gardening is an enjoyable form of relaxation that keeps you active and relieves stress. The benefits of your hard work are beautiful. You can find solace and calm in your garden. Make someone smile by giving them a bouquet of your flowers.

Baking and cooking can help you relax, and the creativity of cooking can help your mind. Delicious tastes and sweet aromas are a plus. Soft music and pleasant lighting will put the final touches on your homemade meal. Mmmmm, delicious!

Puzzles can be a fun way to engage and challenge your brain, and they can also be relaxing. It is a creative form of mental activity. Choose from word puzzles, mathematical puzzles, logic problems, visual puzzles, brain teasers, and much more.

Writing offers a variety of benefits. You can create a whole new world by writing a story, you can organize your thoughts together for nonfiction, or you can record parts of your life through a diary or memoir. Maybe you can even publish a book or article.

A museum is a nice quiet place to visit. Enjoy the exhibitions and collections, and let your mind wander to another place and time. Contemplate a work of art, study a historical artifact, or learn something about science or engineering. Discover something new.

Do you enjoy it when you receive a letter, telephone call, or email from a long-lost friend or acquaintance? If so, you could be the long-lost friend who suddenly reaches out to someone else. Perhaps you will supply a needed ray of sunshine for them.

Hiking and backpacking along trails, fishing, or rowing a boat are great ways to experience the great outdoors. Look, listen, and smell the wonders of nature. Taking photographs allows you to capture the quiet and beautiful scenes so that you may relive them later.

You don't have to go to the ocean, or live in a rain forest, or hike to a bubbling creek to enjoy the sounds of nature. These relaxing sounds, and many others, can be incorporated into playlists made for relaxation and meditation. Just relax.

Colorful Sunsets

5

Rewrite Print in Cursive

Instructions: Rewrite each printed paragraph onto the blank lines below.

If you forget how to write a letter, consult pages vi-vii at the front of the book.

The layout is designed so that you may write on every other line.

See the example below. **Check your answers on pages 107-116.**

Listening to falling raindrops can be

relaxing and help you fall asleep.

Listening to falling raindrops can be

relaxing and help you fall asleep.

The color of every rose has a special meaning. Red roses symbolize true love. Bright yellow roses demonstrate friendship. Pure white roses represent innocence. A lavender rose expresses love at first sight. Pink roses are a symbol of beauty.

Different flowers also have their own symbols. Examples include violets for loyalty, yellow tulips for sunshine, sunflowers for adoration, daffodils for regard, daisies for innocence, rhododendrons for danger, and chrysanthemums for cheerfulness.

Aromatherapy is a practice that uses natural oils extracted from plants and flowers to enhance the health of your mind and body. Essential oils can be inhaled, absorbed through the skin, used during a massage, or added to your bath.

Lavender may calm the mind and body to aid in sleeping. Vanilla may elevate feelings of joy. Orange and ginger may sharpen the senses and release tension. Jasmine may perk your mood. Cinnamon may help sharpen the mind.

When experiencing change, thinking of the metamorphosis of a butterfly may offer hope. Just as the crawling wormlike caterpillar transforms into a colorful flying butterfly, sometimes we must experience changes to experience a beautiful result.

A tree that bends with the wind may become stronger than it would have if it had been tied to a stake. Similarly, sometimes in life, it can help to work with what is around us and to go with the flow. We may be able to adapt well when we can't improve a situation.

People often feel that they are too

busy to meditate. However, when

meditation succeeds in helping your

mind be calm and focused, meditation

may actually free up some valuable

time. Fifteen minutes of meditation a

day may be enough.

By focusing one's mind on the present, one can temporarily escape distracting or stressful thoughts. A meditating person might focus on breathing, on repeating sounds, or on body sensations. Meditation can be a fairly simple yet rewarding activity.

Recreational activities can benefit

both the mind and the body. Do you

enjoy jogging, aerobics, jumping jacks,

yoga, push-ups, dancing, tennis, golf,

ping pong, basketball, softball, soccer,

racquetball, swimming, skiing, hiking,

or something else?

Even leisurely activities like walking

can help to provide regular exercise.

There are many places to walk, such

as strolling through a park, hiking

along a trail, walking around a mall,

or taking a dog out for a walk. How

much do you walk each week?

Can you remember the last time that you gazed out into the stars on a clear night? Nature offers many wonders that are easy to take for granted. Do you remember wondering about the moon, sun, planets, and stars when you were a child?

Children tend to be curious. Try to remember what it was like to be a child, discovering something for the first time that you now take for granted. Kids find wonder in simple tasks like tying shoes, interesting phrases, and different types of objects.

Getting involved in arts and crafts is one way to feel creative. Express your imagination by drawing, painting, sculpting, building, designing, molding, decorating, coloring, paper folding, engraving, repurposing, or refurbishing, for example.

Museums and art galleries let you explore a variety of creations and achievements. Exhibits may impress, inspire, or motivate you, and you may discover something new. You won't know what they have to offer until you explore them.

Imagine what it was like to live in the past with much less technology: traveling by horse or train, mailing handwritten letters, reading by candlelight, not having television or radio, and kids using their imagination to play games.

There may have been fewer distractions when there was less technology, but there was also less convenience and fewer medical options. Taking an occasional break from technology can help to experience the benefits of both worlds.

What positive words can you think of?

Here are some examples: sunshine,

smiley face, hope, confident, sweet,

fun, exciting, bright, calm, amazing,

fantastic, and upbeat. Reading your

personal list of positive words may

help give you a lift when you need it.

What's on your mind? Grab a pen and paper. Psychologists have found that writing down your thoughts and feelings may help to relieve stress and help you feel better. People who write down their goals tend to accomplish more.

 Good Times

6

Writing Prompts

Instructions: These writing prompts offer practice writing in cursive.

If you forget how to write a letter, consult pages vi-vii at the front of the book.

The layout is designed so that you may write on every other line.

1. Make a list of happy words.

2. Describe an activity that you enjoy doing.

3. Describe a place that you enjoy visiting.

4. Describe a sport that you enjoy.

5. Describe a person. (It can be any person.)

6. *List things that help you relax.*

_____
_____
_____
_____
_____
_____
_____
_____
_____
_____

7. *List things that you would like to do some day.*

_____
_____
_____
_____
_____
_____
_____
_____
_____
_____

8. List things that you enjoyed doing as a child.

9. List things that you enjoy doing now.

10. How do you feel about learning cursive?

_____
_____
_____
_____
_____
_____
_____
_____
_____
_____

11. How was your day today?

_____
_____
_____
_____
_____
_____
_____
_____
_____

12. How would you like the weather to be tomorrow?

_____
_____
_____
_____
_____
_____
_____
_____

13. How do you hope to be five years from now?

_____
_____
_____
_____
_____
_____
_____
_____

14. Explain something special that you can do.

_____
_____
_____
_____
_____
_____
_____
_____
_____
_____

15. Explain something interesting that you know.

_____
_____
_____
_____
_____
_____
_____
_____
_____
_____

16. Explain something you learned recently.

17. Explain something you learned long ago.

18. Describe a house that you lived in.

_____

_____

_____

_____

_____

_____

_____

_____

_____

_____

19. Describe a school that you attended.

_____

_____

_____

_____

_____

_____

_____

_____

_____

_____

20. Describe a news event that you remember.

21. Describe a celebrity of your choice.

22. Describe a fond memory that you have.

23. Describe yourself (to someone you just met).

24. Describe a city that you would like to visit.

25. Describe what an ideal day would be like.

26. Summarize a book that you read.

27. Summarize an experience that you once had.

28. Write one sentence beginning with each letter of the alphabet.

 Wonderful

Answers to Part 5

Page 65:

Listening to falling raindrops can be relaxing and help you fall asleep.

Page 66:

The color of every rose has a special meaning. Red roses symbolize true love. Bright yellow roses demonstrate friendship. Pure white roses represent innocence. A lavender rose expresses love at first sight. Pink roses are a symbol of beauty.

Page 67:

Different flowers also have their own symbols. Examples include violets for loyalty, yellow tulips for sunshine, sunflowers for adoration, daffodils for regard, daisies for innocence, rhododendrons for danger, and chrysanthemums for cheerfulness.

Page 68:

Aromatherapy is a practice that uses natural oils extracted from plants and flowers to enhance the health of your mind and body. Essential oils can be inhaled, absorbed through the skin, used during a massage, or added to your bath.

Page 69:

Lavender may calm the mind and body to aid in sleeping. Vanilla may elevate feelings of joy. Orange and ginger may sharpen the senses and release tension. Jasmine may perk your mood. Cinnamon may help sharpen the mind.

Page 70:

When experiencing change, thinking of the metamorphosis of a butterfly may offer hope. Just as the crawling wormlike caterpillar transforms into a colorful flying butterfly, sometimes we must experience changes to experience a beautiful result.

Page 71:

A tree that bends with the wind may become stronger than it would have if it had been tied to a stake. Similarly, sometimes in life, it can help to work with what is around us and to go with the flow. We may be able to adapt well when we can't improve a situation.

Page 72:

People often feel that they are too busy to meditate. However, when meditation succeeds in helping your mind be calm and focused, meditation may actually free up some valuable time. Fifteen minutes of meditation a day may be enough.

Page 73:

By focusing one's mind on the present, one can temporarily escape distracting or stressful thoughts. A meditating person might focus on breathing, on repeating sounds, or on body sensations. Meditation can be a fairly simple yet rewarding activity.

Page 74:

Recreational activities can benefit both the mind and the body. Do you enjoy jogging, aerobics, jumping jacks, yoga, push-ups, dancing, tennis, golf, ping pong, basketball, softball, soccer, racquetball, swimming, skiing, hiking, or something else?

Page 75:

Even leisurely activities like walking can help to provide regular exercise. There are many places to walk, such as strolling through a park, hiking along a trail, walking around a mall, or taking a dog out for a walk. How much do you walk each week?

Page 76:

Can you remember the last time that you gazed out into the stars on a clear night? Nature offers many wonders that are easy to take for granted. Do you remember wondering about the moon, sun, planets, and stars when you were a child?

Page 77:

Children tend to be curious. Try to remember what it was like to be a child, discovering something for the first time that you now take for granted. Kids find wonder in simple tasks like tying shoes, interesting phrases, and different types of objects.

Page 78:

Getting involved in arts and crafts is one way to feel creative. Express your imagination by drawing, painting, sculpting, building, designing, molding, decorating, coloring, paper folding, engraving, repurposing, or refurbishing, for example.

Page 79:

Museums and art galleries let you explore a variety of creations and achievements. Exhibits may impress, inspire, or motivate you, and you may discover something new. You won't know what they have to offer until you explore them.

Page 80:

Imagine what it was like to live in the past with much less technology: traveling by horse or train, mailing handwritten letters, reading by candlelight, not having television or radio, and kids using their imagination to play games.

Page 81:

There may have been fewer distractions when there was less technology, but there was also less convenience and fewer medical options. Taking an occasional break from technology can help to experience the benefits of both worlds.

Page 82:

What positive words can you think of? Here are some examples: sunshine, smiley face, hope, confident, sweet, fun, exciting, bright, calm, amazing, fantastic, and upbeat. Reading your personal list of positive words may help give you a lift when you need it.

Page 83:

What's on your mind? Grab a pen and paper. Psychologists have found that writing down your thoughts and feelings may help to relieve stress and help you feel better. People who write down their goals tend to accomplish more.

Hammock Time

Advanced Cursive Handwriting Practice Workbook for Teens

Butterfly Cursive Handwriting Practice Workbook

More Handwriting Workbooks by Julie Harper

wackysentences.com

amazon.com/author/julieharper

- Cursive Handwriting Practice Workbook for Teens

- Advanced Cursive Handwriting Practice Workbook for Teens

- Wacky Sentences Handwriting Workbook

- Cursive Handwriting Practice Workbook for Boys

- Butterfly Cursive Handwriting Practice Workbook

- Cursive Handwriting Workbook for Girls

- Save the Earth Cursive Handwriting Practice Workbook

- Flower Cursive Handwriting Practice Workbook

- Letters, Words, and Silly Phrases Handwriting Workbook

- Spooky Cursive Handwriting Practice Workbook

- Friendship Cursive Handwriting Practice Workbook

Made in the USA
Monee, IL
03 July 2020